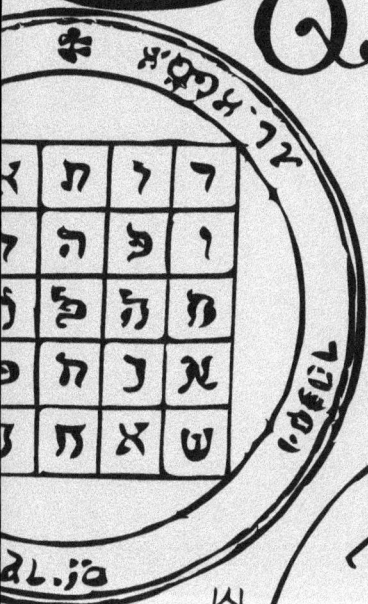
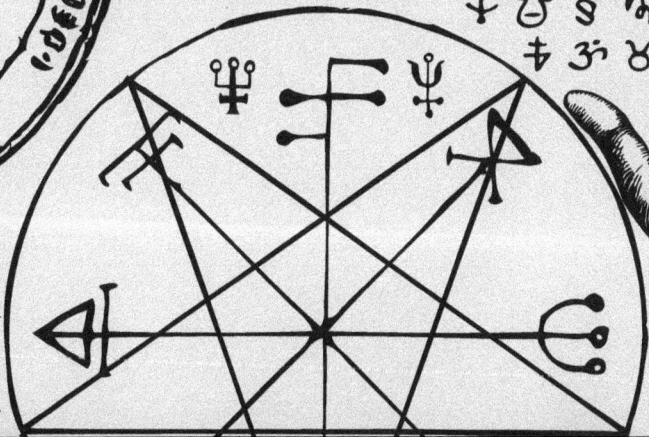
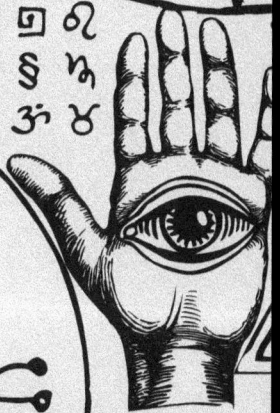

Also by Matthew Kosinski

Transformation Sequence (Ghost City Press, 2020)

Alone in the White Marble City (New Delta Review, 2020)

Seven Times Obstructed by Flame (Ghost City Press, 2019)

Your Human Shape

_____

Kosinski

ISBN: 978-1-915079-12-1

Cover designed by Aaron Kent

Edited and typeset by Aaron Kent

Broken Sleep Books Ltd
Rhydwen,
Talgarreg,
SA44 4HB
Wales

Contents

We being everything, wherefore the necessity
of imagining we are not?

- Austin Osman Spare,
The Book of Pleasure: The Psychology of Ecstasy

Your Human Shape

Matthew Kosinski

Note on the Text

The Lesser Key of Solomon is a 17th-century grimoire containing descriptions of 72 spirits purportedly sealed in a bronze vessel by the biblical King Solomon, alongside relevant conjuration instructions.

Your Human Shape reimagines *The Lesser Key* as a poetic text. Each poem's dedication references one of Solomon's spirits. The individual poems serve as incantatory objects, sigils through which the spirits might manifest during the encounter between text and reader.

To quote Aleister Crowley, "The spirits of [the *Key*] are portions of the human brain."

The Right-Hand Book of Stock Photography

For Dantalion

Hey this wheat
field shimmered
straight to gold status.
Is this how
the ache of empire
operates? When you put
white people in a fever
dream
house it's solar-powered.

It isn't that the stars
have started falling
for our benefit.
It's that location
is for the poor.
This tableau in relief
against Las Vegas
or the Colosseum.
Why not both?
dad asks through
a mouthful of squid ink.

I mean you can either vote
for family values
or drape a Soviet flag
over the lower forty-eight.
See inset for Alaska and
Hawaii.
Having not cracked
geography entirely just yet,
the strategy is to hyperlink
and rain glitter down
quick. The khaki comes
on strong like Charybdis'
puckered asshole watermaw.

Some existences linger on long after the death of the thing itself.

This archive
dislocates my subject.
Each photograph
furnished with p-zombies.
My consciousness clicks
into the slots of their lacks.
This is what I call
a hard problem.
The redness of their wine
shares a redness with mine,
though a screen is nothing
if not equivocal.

Similitude only poses an issue
as long as you address it.
Noumenon, from
Greek νοούμενο,
"to think, to mean."
As in I can grip a kite string
but the ultimate kite
escapes me, in fact
refuses me by its very nature,
the essence shrouded
on the far side of its image,
as are all the people waving.

Negotiations break down
approaching the thing-in-it-
self.
The front end accordions
against what appears
to be horizon.
But of my vessel-objects,
how do all their faces
know to look away?

Extinction-Level Event

For Marbas

I admit I
have been passing my days
in a strange manner.
My problems
were not too serious
until the radiologist
yelled at me for breathing.
Now our galaxy's magnetic field
is all askew, and Google
has censored the photographs.
Our self-proclaimed top minds
are on it when they are not
hacking celebrities' phones.
One day all our nudes
will be in the public domain.
The stage magician bears
his assistant who agrees
to bare a midriff because
the ticket price is high.
Her head disappears inside a box.

Everything happens at all times, though exceedingly slowly.

This next call will be
the disaster call,
like pushing a nose
through someone's face
in a failed attempt
at self-defense.
What about a garlic clove
skin? What about the ACLU?
Oh, sure, selling your labor
power is common sense
but tell everyone you cast
a healing spell
for the two-year-old
with rhabdomyosarcoma
and you're the bad guy?
nine in ten theoreticians agree:
when it's time to rally support
for the New World Order
they'll stage first contact,
but we've already had it.

I Have Thrown My Stasis Body to the Pyre Already

For Leraikha

We are living in the Occupied Northeast he says, referring to gun laws. He has a military fuck fetish. His preferred porno includes crisis actors. His phantom limb packs heat. It gives great handjobs, too. I shot into its palm; it was that warm. I took it as shelter from death. Rain beat on the school roof like arrows. I have noticed that semen sort of suppurates when you come. This shouldn't be an omen.

I wanted to preserve us from the stink and flaming breath. Light enters through the eye; it refracts through the wound. Necrosis actually constructs. You can't build a house without rupturing some space. All that space wants a subject to populate itself. I tell you my hilarious philosopher's joke: to know is to turn away under duress. Close the door. You weren't raised in a barn.

GiGi, a special collection by Gigi Hadid for Tommy Hilfiger. Full-body advertisement on the side of a newsstand shows her in naval color scheme, a strafe of black buttons across her left hip. Reminds one how impossible it is to not take damage. We need the air strikes; the climate map projects a Boston archipelago. But this peacoat is perfect for my danger body. God grant me the serenity, etc.

As If Looking Up
For Gaap

My president's
name is Gaap.
His office is
to make men
ignorant and
insensible.
Following
my endoscopy
the nurse
wheeled me
into the
recovery bay.
Gaap climbed
onto my
gurney and
put his ear to
my stomach.
No, no, Gaap
said. I'm
afraid it's all
inflamed.
This conflicted
with my
doctor's report.
I looked up
as if from a
shallow firepit.

He
conducts
himself
humanly.

This bed is very small. For both of us to fit, we must cradle one another.

Fact-check
your tongue.
Is that an
apple seed
or cyanide?
The answer
is usually the
worse one.
Fact-check
your haptics.
Whose body
is below yours
and how did
they get there?
Eminent
domain
doesn't count.
Fact-check
your tax
documents.
When the
armored truck
rolls through
your ward, ask
for a rebate.
Terminate
the contract.

Uses for Teeth
For Botis

The women gather to stare
into each other's mouths.
The first woman hands a tissue
to the second woman.
The second woman holds tissue
up next to her face and smiles.
The third woman lays
a dress out on the hotel bed
and it rots. The fourth erases
every last shred of evidence
that she has ever existed.
She is going underground.
A voiceover assures us her
teeth will be 25 times whiter
when she resurfaces.
The fifth woman is detained
by sexy French border guards
who don't believe
it's her face on the passport.

In the mouth of my president, an interrobang.

My other president's name is Botis.
He's an ugly sonofabitch.
He shows up to the annual street fair
in a snakeskin tuxedo and
pulls the children aside to tell them
"The king cobra only eats other snakes.
That's why he's the king."
This wins him reelection every four years.
We never have a different president.
The day my father took me to see Botis
he sobbed and sobbed in the ice cream
parlor afterward. He said I had learned
the most valuable lesson. He said
Botis is a great [redacted] because
no one is quite sure what Botis is.
Eventually biologists gave Botis his own
taxonomic domain. It's a question mark.
Later that night I caught my father trying
to fit his own feet into his mouth.

An Hurtful Angel

For Astaroth

How long
have we stood
in line for this
peepshow? In a waste
-land of ecstasy,
each tepid atom
in its cocoon of self
-love. Mutated
fruit flies
with eyes for legs.
Rows and rows
of clean unopened
boxes on the shelves.
A truly inspired use
of sacred geometry:
The floor plan
channels all
psychic energy
through the
cash register.
How to keep
a people hungry
and hidebound.
Cross-legged
at the center
emitting a low and
steady aum is a pig
in his tie and tails.

Dire straits
direct the eye
and the ear
toward the public
square. You cannot
turn a poem
into a protest.
All differences are
reconciled through
body language.
People keep
climbing the stairs
but at the top
a man shoves
them back down.
The papers
treat it like a fall.
Think: reaching for
that baddest apple.
Think: Old Scratch,
who ultimately
lost his privileges
because he demanded
a little more slop for
the cosmic dog bowl.
Solidarity means
you get one
and you get one.

Who is the slayer of your gods but a god? Kingdoms are their own despoilers.

Ghost Opening Its Shirt
For Murmur

Would you do me a kindness
and quit dying on the internet
in front of me? I am petitioning
the gods I believe in:
Ghost ex machina;
ghost opening its shirt
as a metaphor for power;
five hundred and fifty Tiffany lamps
that shatter into the stupid night.
Inheritance powder was
a euphemism for poison
in seventeenth-century France.
Now when Grandpa dies
two people arrive in trench coats

[We cannot be too careful in our choice, for it determines the body we inhabit.]

to shower you with medical debt,
paperwork like cherry blossom petals
raining over a cinematically
recreated cobblestone street.
I am so thankful to be alive
in the U. S. of A.
where our souls have access
to vast lines of credit
taken out in our children's names.
Still, the committee keeps deciding
not to grant an award this year.
All that work for nothing.
Well "yes, and"
is the key to good improv, you know.

Agency Report: Post-Exorcism Floralosis, Its Characteristics, and Its Causes
For Buer

Following an exorcism,
you may smell flowers.
This is a common
and harmless side effect,
though the agency
does not yet understand
the mechanism by which it is caused.
Investigation is ongoing.

> [*Tie barley straw around a rock and throw it
> into a river or lake while visualizing any pain you have.*]

One prominent theory, first proposed by an occult podcast host
and circulated widely by amateur demonologists, holds that
post-exorcism floralosis is a byproduct of planar rebalancing.
According to the hypothesis, demonic encounters can be
understood as psychic near-death experiences. The emergence
of a demonic entity into human space produces
a surge of thanatopic energy, which tilts the existential scale
toward quietus. However, the human plane tends toward
metaphysical equilibrium. Thus, the entity's expulsion spurs
a cosmic correction, producing an equal but opposite surge of erotic energy,
thereby reestablishing planar balance. The host argues this erotic surge emits
a flowery scent because spring is traditionally associated
with life, rebirth, and the bloom of flowers.

The agency rejects the host's theory on the grounds it is unscientific and ridiculous.

Post-exorcism floralosis presents an additional puzzle regarding
the identification of the particular flower(s) whose scent(s)
the exorcism evokes. Here, as in the matter of the aroma's genesis,
available data is inconclusive. By collating sensory descriptions
provided by interview subjects with a list of herbs commonly used
in exorcism rituals, the agency has determined
the following plants are most likely implicated in the matter:

Sea mayweed
Fragrance profile: Phantom chamomile

Feverwort
Fragrance profile: Floral lace runner across the center
of a farm table set for a semiformal occasion

Clove
Fragrance profile: Sharp and aphrodisiac

Solomon's seal
Fragrance profile: An invasive species of heavens

Disgrace Magic
For Raum

What follows is:
I fall upon the (t)horns
of life; I poke a finger
at the gash; my whole
hand slips in. I sink
up to my elbow in myself.
This is the field of action
dominates you.
This is whittling a tiny
Solomon figurine
to deposit in the gash.
This is smuggling
that figurine
through a hole
in the fence. This is
removing that figurine
from your gut and
igniting it. This is
lobbing that figurine
through a window.
This is maybe it detonates.
This is who is the target?

Acceptable forms of disgrace magic
and news feed contents 1/29/17:

Smoking organic cigarettes
while you practice energy healing.

Gunking up your computer brain
with J-pop dance routines.

Military raid in which
an eight-year-old child dies.
Her red tutu spills out of her neck
to configure the seal of Raum.

[The creator gave us certain dignities
by rendering us in his image.]

Wolfing pickles before bed
and rubbing salt on your lips but
you still can't astral project.

[Is it any wonder in this climate?]

It has become inborn and your body is sensitive.

Has the world not ever been bloody?

Always a Tank
For Valefar

We saw
the Total Television
assimilate each of us
into its tricky tissue.
Our simulacra

must involve
a certain amount of corpse.
The only legitimate dissent
regards the minimum
nonzero number.

One neon face said
"THERE IS A TANK
PRESSING DOWN
ON A GLOBE
-SPANNING CHEST."

There is always a tank
and often tank enough.

Iron and fire could not refrain from accomplishing our will.

Option one:
Nightmare legion
of bloodeaters
on the dole.

Option two:
An orderly procession of
full plates around
the smithereened table.

Option three:
Make a throne
of the tank
and corpses.

Option four:
Doves are considered
property and thus
thievable by all
the usual means.

Fiat/Fiat/Fiat

For Bifrons

Who binds and loosens the fetters of this body which mortifies the soul?

The plan was
to take on as much debt
as possible and off myself
in the Queens-Midtown Tunnel
but my trigger
discipline is too good.
The world is so full
of garbage I can't be petty
anymore. I get something
in my eye every
time we hang out. My brother
may have a better credit score
but his teeth are worse
than mine, so tell me:
Who is the joke really on?

To light what seem like candles
upon the graves of the dead:
To follow a friar's lantern
to the flea market
swamps and surrender
this complex to the trash fair:
to bring the excommunicated
back into the fold
through a High Magick terrorism:
to ring a bell: to close a book:
to dash their candles on the ground:
but the wilderness
is the buffet of honey
and locusts: the feast
less opulent than the fast.

Most Perfect Case
For Samigina

In the company of a priest
named Giles and a girl
named Isabeau, Villon met
a Breton whom he beat to death
with a stone. Then followed
two thefts. Then nothing.
There were poems in between.
He may have died on a gallows
in a quaint French town.

Esclarmonde de Foix became
a Cathar once her husband died.
She reached a perfect state,
renounced the flesh garment.
There is debate about her life.
The Catholics hold her heretic.
She established schools
and hospitals in Occitania.
Then the crusade escalated.

Agency Report: Concerning the Old Man Sat Atop a Crocodile

For Agares

Section I

Reported to Biloxi PD at 4:56 PM CDT on 3.24.2017. Caller described "an old fair Man, riding upon a Crocodile, carrying a Goshawk upon his fist, yet mild in appearance" emerging from the gulf waters directly outside of Margaritaville Resort. Two officers were dispatched to the scene. [NOTE: In the course of the investigation, the agency has learned of Biloxi PD's unwritten but strictly observed "Margaritaville Resort Protocol": Before responding to any calls from the resort, the department draws straws. The two officers who draw the shortest straws receive the assignment. The agency could bring this matter to the attention of certain state- and/or federal-level regulatory bodies to commence disciplinary procedures but has declined to do so on the grounds that the agency, too, would hesitate to interact with anyone who would willingly stay in a Jimmy Buffet-themed resort, regardless of whether or not they were the victim of some heinous crime.] Upon arrival, officers found the old Man sat atop his Crocodile, with the promised Goshawk upon his fist, waiting on the resort's dock. The officers were initially skeptical this was the same old Man who had been reported. Whereas the caller described her old Man as "fair" and "mild in appearance," the officers agreed they would describe this old Man as "pasty" and "slightly perturbed." Caller was not on the scene to confirm, nor had the old Man attracted a crowd. [NOTE: Considering this event occurred at Margaritaville Resort, the agency is unsurprised the old Man drew no crowd. In fact, the agency is genuinely astonished that any of the resort's guests had taken enough notice to place a call to Biloxi PD in the first place.] [NOTE TO PRIOR NOTE: See Section II for a possible explanation.] Officers approached the old Man and initiated conversation. A transcript, taken from audio captured by the officers' bodycams, follows:

Officer A: Good evening, sir.

Old Man: (Earthquake noises)

Officer A: You, uh, you understand why we're here today, don't you?

Old Man: (Earthquake noises)

Officer A: Would you mind telling us what's going on?

(Extended silence)

Officer B: Sir, I'm going to have to ask you to comply with the request.

Officer A: Would you, uh, can you tell us what you're doing with that crocodile?

Old Man: (Earthquake noises)

Officer A: Right, but you understand why the guests aren't too happy about this, right?

Old Man: (Earthquake noises)

Officer B: Is that crocodile an endangered species?

Officer A: Or the bird? Is the bird protected?

Old Man: (Earthquake noises)

Officer B: I'm not entirely – I'm not following what you mean by that, but I believe threatening an officer of the law's spiritual and temporal dignity counts as assaulting an officer.

Officer A: I guarantee we could get a prosecutor to file those charges.

(Extended silence.)

Old Man: (All languages and tongues presently at once)

It is unclear what occurred following this portion of the conversation. No footage is available of the event beyond this moment, as the officers claim their bodycams failed. The officers themselves are unwilling or unable to describe the encounter any further. Other members of Biloxi PD can only recount that the officers returned to the station at approximately noon CDT on 3.25.2017. There were no other witnesses to the encounter, nor has the initial caller been identified. No additional sightings have been reported. Agency investigation is ongoing.

Preliminary conclusion: Possible End of Days scenario,
considering the range of the American Crocodile is limited to Southern Florida.

Section II

While the agency strongly believes
this event may represent an End of Days scenario,
this is a controversial conclusion.
Indeed, a not insignificant minority of the agency
believes this may have been a publicity stunt
put on by Margaritaville Resort. The inability
of either officer, or any member of Biloxi PD
for that matter, to account for what occurred
following the recorded portion of the conversation
with the old Man gives this minority pause,
as does the suggestion that any of
Margaritaville Resort's clientele would
wrench themselves away from their miserable daiquiris
long enough to notice an old Man riding a Crocodile
and carrying a Goshawk. Note, again, that the old Man
is said to have attracted no crowd whatsoever.
The minority also objects to the claim that a guest
of the resort would be of the mien to describe
the old Man as "mild of appearance,"
much less know what a Goshawk is.
As it stands, the agency itself had to look that one up.

[*I have all the health, and treasure, and logic I need. I have no time to waste.*]

When the Breeders Came

For Sitri

Take me to the leader
of your exotic dance fitness class.
A girl's gotta work on her riot muscles.
If you can't see
anything it means you're
surrounded. They called it
"Project Thor" and
they called it "Rods from God."
            So as not to violate
        the treaty they would drop
twenty-foot tungsten poles from space
        with enough force to annihilate
            nuclear bunkers in Russia.
            Your honor, it's not a war
        -crime, it's a loophole. Anything is
possible if you apply yourself.
A want is a crater someone else blew
in you to fill back up
with stone. Desire, however, generates.
The way a lamp produces light.
The way a door opens.

            Aphrodite lifts her leg
        above the bathtub rim and
runs her hands down her calves
            as if advertising
a disposable razor. Her father
    was a set of severed genitals;
        her mother was sea foam.
    And they say capital is irrational.
A smog rolls in
from the financial sector,
which is how shadow people get born.
They swarm. All reality aspires to the
condition of their cut physiques,
which, when grasped,
disperse. It hurts to watch, aches
            more not to touch. Listening
        to simulated rain on my laptop
            while rain falls outside.
I don't know what came from the sky but
            my needs keep proliferating,
            putting on this human shape.

    [Are you the creator or just yourself as you fondly imagine your contents?]

Biomassive Black Hole

For Barbatos

The skull wrapped in a red bow
marks where you died
the last time around and the last

When you find everything
you came here for
kneel and let the black wolf

These fox
ears make you
invincible

Two thousand pounds' worth
of spiders could eat
a two-hundred-pound man in one

Dredging a corner you missed
previously / here is a dog /
here is someone's child / this sewer

Huge Revolutionary Body
For Zepar

[and by the dreadful judgments of GOD, and by the uncertain Sea of Glass,
I do potently exorcise thee.]

disregarding   all   research
and   quantitative   education
ordinary to the IQ of failure
nothing   to   solve
limit   of   ability   to   answer
question   still   healthy
out of business most taboo
the   empty   suits
what   we   owe(d)

the clash at the center of red
a   system   of   prophecy
humanely   determined
the   governor   gifts   us
the very knife the landed
gentry   went   into   hiding
action   triggers   scripture
the   rest   is   liberalism

*[In fact, heresy is one huge revolutionary body having as its object
chaos and corruption.]*

Big Holler in Megiddo's Direction

For Phenex

Bird is a grief
in a black ribbon
necktie. It wants
to suck the meat
out of their
many genders
and their ways of
loving and fucking.
The way I want
to suck rifles
out of the exit
– can you ever
feel bad enough
to stop posting
video talismans?
A perfect yoga
posture
could save
this world
or put a body
to this viol.

There is no effect which is truly and necessarily miraculous.

How dare you
align yourselves
with the blueness
of the sky
and the blueness
of trouble music?
A priest sees
a way in all of this
to build a new
guitar factory,
to line it with
black sandbags.
But there is
something beyond
our immediate
humanity.
All this devil talk
points to
a big wet button
we push
to get free.

In terms of what can't:

In terms of what can be sung:

Hot Mess
For Amon

A man with dogteeth
walks his cloud of ravens. Do
you find this erotic?
The pleasure of relation
with desire foregrounded.

I wouldn't ask anything
of you that I wouldn't also ask of
the dogtoothed man.

Come touch me
slightly and fade.

How hot is it
that he produces fire
between his canines?

How hot is a dissipating chord between dogteeth? Daddy's circumstance is spoilage.

It's rarely
the first iteration
that lasts.

It's rare,
the first iteration.

A child wails
in many intervals.
Harmonically
as in a chord,

which dissipates.

Daddy, pick me up.
Daddy, put me
down.

Build a Tower

For Sabnok

I was hunting for cultural Marxists when I
found my own bent spine / A state opera
-tive had been keeping it in a large me
-dical icebox like the type they tr
-ansport organs in / The icebox
had been lodged in the bran
-ches of a tree in the park
overlooking Hoboken /
This explained so
much / My scol
-iosis was a ma
-ndate I had
not assent
-ed to

It took baby several years to achieve his dr
-eam of working in sports / Then he dr
-ave some sort of topless vehicle st
-raight into the Hudson / That is
also a kind of dream / What if
this is the dumbest machine
we've ever built / What if
we've broken our conf
-ines / Who exactly
is the mayor of
the skyline
rising up
ahead
of us

Build a tower / Steal treasure out of kings' pockets / Which / Soles rotten / Lron-Worm

Crush and Gift
For Asmoday

Dragons are convenient
until we let them do
all the work.
Throw the cloak;
find a machine. One man
ordered another
to pull the lever.
He did and the lights
went out across Kentucky.

The texts say nothing
of us. Still, the land
reaches its fever pitch.
Compare the melthaze
cast upward by
hot tar in August.

I never asked for
this phossy jaw, but I earned its
greenwhite smolder.

When the exorcist hath a mind to call him, let it be abroad, and let him stand on his feet.

You and I have a treasure
which comprises
a field of empty
crosses adjacent
the New Jersey Turnpike.

We are meant to thread them
with grapevines
because grapes remain
useful regardless

of how we treat them.
When you crush
a grape beneath your bootheel,
give it time and fungus.
Call it by another name.

(Stick that
in your utopia
and smoke it.)

In the Burning Chamber

For Focalor

The technology is there.
We could upgrade every cop
with driptorches to make
their function more obvious.
Law is a prescribed burn
by other means. And the people,
caught, do catch
fire: in the flash of it
appearing quite like martyrs.
The trouble is in hashing
out what they index.
The legislature claims
it's evidence in favor
of toppling the welfare state
and installing a series
of puppet inquisitors
at designated checkpoints.
I'd object but
I'm already in contempt.

He said you could burn
one thousand cigarettes
and   kill   no   one.
He said you could burn
one gallon of gasoline
and   kill   everyone.
I said I think there is
some sleight of hand
at   work   here.

It's unfortunate, really,
that one can no longer trust
one's dentist to be a pillar
of the community. Mine
is stricken with Stendhal's
by the curve of my incisor.
She says she needs it
for a black mass. She says
she'll give it right back.
Next a hygienist
sweeps in chanting
the depth measurements
of my periodontal pockets.
It only conjures anxiety.
She powerwashes
my mouth with
a high-end water jet.
I wonder if I am
supposed to swallow.

The inquisitors
arrange themselves industriously
and with no hard feelings.
They get triple time for this.
They don't kill unless spoken to.
At least that's how the chief
justice has it, though he has it
on hearsay, though
it all becomes semantics
when the majority opinion
namechecks L'affaire des poisons.

Under the Ancien Régime
they threaded strips of cloth
down the condemned's throat
and posed the question
– rhetorical, of course:
One gallon or two?
U.S. soldiers some centuries later
named it the water cure.
You had to drink to keep from drowning.
What happened to the stomach
was a separate matter entirely.

Agency Report: An Evaluation of Paimon's Claims Concerning the Origins of the Earth
For Paimon

Context:

Having made very little progress in deciphering the true nature of reality, the Department for Research of Ontological and Societal Structures (D.R.O.S.S.) filed a petition (FILING DATE: 10.3.2016) with the Governing Executive Inquisitors' Syndical Trust (G.E.I.S.T.) for permission to conjure Goetic spirit No. 9 / Goetic king No. 2 Paimon (REQUESTED CONJURATION DATE: 11.1.2016). As of 10.31.2016, D.R.O.S.S. had not yet received a response to its petition.[1] So as not to miss 11.1.2016's auspicious lunar aspect, D.R.O.S.S.'s leadership committee decided to summon Paimon regardless.

Successful conjuration occurred at 3 P.M. EDT on 11.1.2016. in the staff kitchen.[2] D.R.O.S.S. reports following the conjuration ritual according to S.O.P. as outlined in *The Lesser Key* with no planned modifications or extemporaneous alterations.

D.R.O.S.S. reports that Paimon appeared in the form of a semi-opaque white mist. His attendants, Goetic sub-spirits Nos. 1 and 2, Labal and Abalim, appeared in the form of two solid gold but mobile capuchin monkeys. D.R.O.S.S. reports they remained silent for the duration of the conversation.

1. While G.E.I.S.T.'s silence on the matter was initially attributed to bureaucratic sluggishness, it has since come to light that G.E.I.S.T. never received D.R.O.S.S.'s petition because G.E.I.S.T. itself cannot be located. Investigations into G.E.I.S.T.'s whereabouts are ongoing. Investigations are also slow going, as agency personnel, when interviewed on the matter, respond with lengthy (and, for the record, sophomoric) soliloquies regarding the nature of "spirit" as an abstract concept. Memos urging agency personnel to take the question literally have been ineffective.

2. D.R.O.S.S. has been formally disciplined for this health code violation.

Claim: It's a joke, actually, and it's still being told. We're posted up around some deitic punchbowl when one of the higher orders – I can't remember who – asks, "What do you get when you cross an elephant and a rhinoceros?" [Pause.] "Elephino!" The earth spontaneously emerged from the enunciation of the punchline, and as soon as this guy is done saying it, it's over.

Evaluation: While the epistemic slipperiness of a joke does seem appropriate to our cosmic situation, this particular joke presents a problematic origin in that it presupposes the existence of elephants and rhinoceroses which, as far as the agency can tell, didn't come into being until the earth itself came along.

Claim: Out of the punchbowl, actually. Not the joke. My mistake. The joke is a different thing entirely. One of the higher orders – again, can't remember which one, they all sort of blur together and might actually all be the same guy – reaches his hand in, prestidigitates a little, and brings this tiny ball of order out of the vast chaotic abyss.

Evaluation: Given the irrationality of our governing structures both physical and meta-, one wonders how this world could possibly be considered a "tiny ball of order." One could make the free will argument, but by virtue of the transitive property, the constituents of the overarching order should themselves be orderly.

Claim: Sorry, sorry. It wasn't the guy. It was a small clay person whom the guy made prior to the party. The guy says, "Watch this," and sets the clay person to swimming around in the punchbowl. The clay person dives down to the bottom of the bowl and surfaces a little later with some undissolved punch mix particles in her hands. She does this over and over again until she has this huge mound of punch mix particles, which she proceeds to form into habitable land.

Evaluation: If one of us made the earth, our preposterous condition would be an appropriate outcome. Pessimistically, this would also mean it's all our fault. Optimistically, this would mean the state of affairs is revocable.

Claim: That all happened, but it was all just the lead-up. Some of the other higher orders got sick of this one guy monopolizing the conversation with all his party tricks. An altercation arose. A physical one. They hacked the guy to pieces. They threw the guy's head into the sky, where it became the moon. His heart became the sun. His bones became people. His brains, the earth. And so on and so forth.

Evaluation: Millennia of human existence do suggest that borderline miraculous things often happen under extreme duress.

Moral Doctrine
For Aim

A string of pearls
emerges from
the Santa Monica Mountains,
enormous and wasteful
but capable of flight,

and

above the Atlantic,
look at all those
tiny nameless islands
— each apparition a
broken chain of lights.

The space between eternal and self, is it not a moral doctrine?

What you've seen
in your life is
a private matter, despite the
handsome bodies of men
who would monetize it,

but

if you could reach
whatever lives
inside those aircraft, you would
forge a stronger
set of links and pull us upward.

A Good Dispute
For Caim

Once we transcend
our physical bodies
we will subsist entirely
on candy-flavored smoke.
For now, there is reason
to believe you can
read sputum as if
it were tea leaves.
The prophet assures
me its aim is true and
its grammar is ripe.
Mucus is the fundamental
building block of life,
which goes a long way
toward explaining the attraction
of transhumanism.
Ditch this sticky wet sock
in favor of a post-everything
(pan)sex(ual) kitten.
Wave your polished
chrome crotch over
the local farmer's market
and watch: Every shopper
turns to coal in the heat
of your ascension.
Bacteria pilots
our weird machines.
It sees an antimicrobial surface
like that and it pops.

Go on discovering the bottomless pit; the bull of the earth has nothing to do with your unclean conscience.

The waters voice
their concerns. Mainly
they tell beachgoers
and oil rigs to screw off
in equal measure.
Sunlight reflects
on the surface of the bay.
Stare long enough
and it resembles pixels
rendering an image.
Each attempt is thwarted;
the screen never loads.
Noise. Busted television snow.
I have seen whole fora
dedicated to thalassophobia:
photo after photo after photo
of the abyssal zone and
its grotesqueries:
teeth with limbs;
tentacular atom bombs;
charts comparing the size
of a diver to the size
of the squid she may encounter.
The ocean spit us out
some 400 million years ago.
When you stare into a womb
it stares back.
Don't write home.
The whole place has changed.

With a Crown Tied About Her Waist
For Gremory

Our Vestal Camgirl felt herself too much swollen with theory.
Tending OUR NATION's pixelated hearth conferred certain privileges,
yes, but what is the point of tool use when it's a purely mental exercise?
Even when two people bucked against their laptops in perfect sync
they would spend themselves into a series of mediating tubes.
Every chat handle belonged to a body somewhere. OUR NATION's
grand new scenario required a collective reincarnation.
Our Camgirl called for materialization, which was her right
as the patron avatar of reproductive labor. If we would not return
to our bodies of our own volition well —

[Thus by hindering belief and semen
they become simple and cosmic.]

She groped for the hem and pulled.
What you may not know
is the bare essence of reality
consists mainly of winds up to 90 MPH.
The Weather Channel's stormchasers,
timid hucksters,
could not screw up the courage
to interview our Camgirl.
Their drones surveilled the local trees,
but not a single one had fallen.
In the city center
all the glassy high-rises vaporized
Standing in the steam of it,
OUR NATION's people blinked,
exposed as raw bone.

Notes

"Extinction-Level Event" quotes *The Book of Pleasure: The Psychology of Ecstasy* by Austin Osman Spare: "Everything happens at all times, though exceedingly slowly."

"An Hurtful Angel" quotes *The Book of Pleasure:* "Who is the slayer of your gods but a god? Kingdoms are their own despoilers."

"Ghost Opening Its Shirt" quotes *The Book of Pleasure:* "We cannot be too careful in our choice, for it determines the body we inhabit."

"Agency Report: Post-Exorcism Floralosis, Its Characteristics, and Its Causes" quotes from a now defucnt online herb grimoire once located at The Magickal Cat: "Tie barley straw around a rock and throw into a river or lake while visualizing any pain you have" and "Steep in red wine for a full cycle of the moon to use as a blood offering. DO NOT DRINK THE WINE."

"Disgrace Magic" quotes from *The Book of Pleasure:* "It has become inborn and your body is sensitive. Has the world not ever been bloody?"

"Always a Tank" paraphrases from *The Key of Solomon the King*, translated by S.L. MacGregor Mathers: "... [L]et the Exorcist be assured that even were they bound with chains of iron, and with fire, they could not refrain from coming to accomplish his will."

"Most Perfect Case" contains a quote often attributed to St. Dominic: "Zeal must be met by zeal, humility by humility, false sanctity by real sanctity." It also paraphrases the apocryphal Christian text *The Vision of Isaiah:* "Who are you, and what is your name, and why are you lifting me up like a bird?" The details regarding the lives of François Villon and Esclarmonde de Foix are sourced from their respective Wikipedia entries.

"Agency Report: Concerning the Old Man Sat Atop a Crocodile" quotes *The Lesser Key of Solomon* as translated by S.L. MacGregor Mathers and Aleister Crowley: "I have all the health, and treasure, and logic I need. I have no time to waste."

"When the Breeders Came" quotes *The Book of Pleasure:* "Are you the creator or just yourself as you fondly imagine your contents?"

"Biomassive Black Hole" was inspired by the lovely little indie video game, *Fear Less!*

"Huge Revolutionary Body" quotes *The Lesser Key of Solomon:* "… [A]nd by the dreadful judgments of GOD, and by the uncertain Sea of Glass, I do potently exorcise thee." It also quotes Montague Summers' introduction to *The Malleus Maleficarum* by Heinrich Kramer and James Sprenger: "In fact, heresy is one huge revolutionary body having as its object chaos and corruption."

"Big Holler in Megiddo's Direction" quotes *The Lesser Key of Solomon:* "There is no effect which is truly and necessarily miraculous."

"Crush and Gift" quotes *The Lesser Key of Solomon*: "When the exorcist hath a mind to call him, let it be abroad, and let him stand on his feet."

"A Moral Doctrine" quotes *The Book of Pleasure:* "The space between eternal and self, is it not a moral doctrine?"

"A Good Dispute" quotes *The Book of Pleasure:* "Go on discovering the Bottomless Pit" and "The Bull of earth has long had nothing to do with your unclean conscience."

"With a Crown Tied About Her Waist" quotes *The Book of Pleasure:* "Thus by hindering belief and semen from conception, they become simple and cosmic."

Acknowledgments

"Always a Tank" first appeared in *Always Crashing*.

"Build a Tower" first appeared in *No, Dear*.

"Extinction-Level Event," "As If Looking Up," "Disgrace Magic," and "Crush and Gift" first appeared in the *Ritual and Capital* anthology from Wendy's Subway.

"An Hurtful Angel" first appeared in *Fence*.

LAY OUT YOUR UNREST

www.ingramcontent.com/pod-product-compliance
Lightning Source LLC
Chambersburg PA
CBHW021944040426
42448CB00008B/1233